Borderline Personality Disorder

How to Communicate and Support Loved
Ones With BPD. Skills to Manage Intense
Emotions & Improve Your Relationship

Linda Hill

Table of Contents

Your Secret Gift #1

Get My Next Book

"Borderline Personality Disorder - Part 2"

(Free for a limited time)

For a limited time, and as a "Thank you" for purchasing this book, you can be added to our "Book 2 Launch List" for free so you get the second book of this series when it gets published (This book will be priced at $24.99 and I guarantee it will be a great read). Simply visit the URL below and follow the instructions. You'll be the first to get it.

Visit here:

lindahillbooks.com/borderline

Scan QR Code:

Your Secret Gift #2

Get the Audio Version for Free

If you would like to get the audio version of this book so you can read along or listen while you are in the car, walking around, or doing other things, you're in luck. For a limited time, I've provided a link that will allow you to download this audiobook for FREE. (This offer may be removed at any time).

Step 1: Go to the URL below.

Step 2: Sign up for the 30-day free-trial membership (You may cancel at any time after, no strings attached)

Step 3: Listen to the audiobook

Visit here:

lindahillbooks.com/bpdpromo

Scan QR Code:

Introduction

Shattering the Mystery of BPD

You look at me and cry, "Everything hurts". I hold you and whisper, "But everything can heal."
–Rupi Kaur

There are two huge misconceptions about Borderline Personality Disorder (BPD) that prevent many people from seeking help when they feel they don't fit into their world the way society says they should. The first is that this is just another branch off the personality disorder tree, relating to toxic or abusive relationships. The other is the stigma that's still placed on mental illness, especially when the condition is a more serious diagnosis. That stigma needs to be shattered, for both the person living with BPD as well as everyone who loves them.

As you'll realize, if you haven't already, BPD is less about an inappropriate personality, and more about being able to control moods and the responses to stressors that trigger those moods. The best place for those who want to help these individuals should begin with having a solid understanding of how most of us handle the usual ups and downs we face in life. For most of us, stress is a natural part of life that we learn to cope with as best as we can. We know that things don't always pan out the way they're planned, and we adapt to surprises, changes, or blips in those plans as best as we can. BPD interferes with this logical process.

Individuals with BPD don't see that gray area most of the rest of us do. We learn at an early age that not everything is black and white. We learn that there is a life beyond our own, and that not everything going on is related to us. Living life based on those black and white extremes is what elicits much of the disappointment BPD sufferers feel.

For example, if a friend doesn't respond immediately to

a text message, there could be many reasons for that: Their phone is shut off, they didn't hear/see the notification, they don't have their phone with them, they're going through something themselves requiring their attention at that moment, etc. These things make sense to us, and we know that person will get back to us eventually. For a person living with BPD, however, they'd think more along the lines of: They don't like me. They're ignoring me. I'm unlovable. I don't deserve friends. For those of us who love a person with BPD, *this* is how they see the world. In order to help them, we need to put ourselves beside them within those extremes that are very real to them. Only then can we guide them to a different way of seeing the world.

A person living with BPD is aware of what's happening inside of them, they just don't understand *why* they do the things they do. If they were able to make that connection, they'd be able to reach out to us before turning to maladaptive ways of coping. Probably the most painful part of this condition, for those of us on the outside looking in, is that they truly don't understand why those around them won't give up on them. If they believe they aren't worth saving, that nothing will help them no matter what options are there, why do we keep trying to help them? Why don't we just give up on them? They don't believe they can be 'fixed,' so why would we keep trying to?

Above everything else, those who love a person with BPD absolutely need to take one point to heart: We don't *fix* people; we *heal* them. People aren't machines that simply need a tweak here or there in order to function properly. People need unconditional love, understanding, support, and guidance. They need the assurance that no matter what they do, say, choose, or how hard they try pushing us away, we will be there. They need to know they aren't defined by any wrong turn they make any more than they're defined by their condition. At least that's how it should be.

It is, at times, an excruciating thing for supporters of individuals with this disorder to walk alongside them, giving their support to a person who may seem not to even want it. Their words will cut deeply, their actions will seem unwarranted and hurtful, and their attempts at keeping us at arms length so we'll give up, make us question, at times, why we don't walk away. We can't.

We won't. Because we know that deep down inside of them, they need us. Maybe not today, or even tomorrow, but the light will go on. And when it does, they'll see we're there and always have been.

The purpose of this book isn't just to arm supporters with knowledge about BPD, and how it affects sufferers. Its other purpose is to support the supporters in seeing the world through the sufferer's eyes. Maybe from that view they'll have some comfort in knowing they aren't alone in their daily battle with a condition they can't see, but know is trying to control their loved one. We may not be able to remove the disorder itself, but we can help our loved one take their power back and be all they're meant to be.

CHAPTER 1

Understanding BPD

One small crack does not mean that you are broken. It means that you were put to the test and you didn't fall apart.

–Linda Poindexter

There are times when we feel that all efforts we make to help someone with a mental or psychological condition are lost. Whether it's an acquaintance, a friend, relative, or significant other, one of the worst feelings is when we *know* something is hurting that person, but have no idea how to save them. We're literally standing by as they're constantly fighting with something that can't be seen, heard, or felt, but it's very real.

The main focus of this chapter is to help those close to

a person with BPD understand the condition a little better. We can't possibly know what they are truly feeling, or why they do the things that they do. What having this knowledge and level of understanding *does* give us is the ability to see how the world may look and feel through their eyes. Having this enables us to think before reacting or responding so that our words or actions *help* rather than *escalate*.

Those who have been a strong supporter of a person with BPD may already be aware of some of this information, but it's always better to have more than to not have enough. We'll start with detailing exactly what BPD is, the specific signs/causes, and when to recognize when something is beyond "intense sadness" or "acting out," and strong indications something is truly wrong that requires professional intervention. Finally, we'll give suggestions on how to be able to tell the difference between BPD and other personality disorders or other conditions with similar symptoms (e.g., bipolar disorder).

No matter how small a supporter may think a sign is initially, it could help with making sure the sufferer is being guided to the best possible path to coping with their condition. It's important to remember that there isn't a 'quick fix' in helping a loved one with BPD. It will take time and a strong sense of knowing that there will be days with great success, and others where many steps are taken backwards. It's all par for the course, and there will be a time when some strategy, or therapeutic method, will finally click. Until that time comes, be as supportive, perseverant, and ever-present as you can be.

They'll remember that above all else.

BPD 101: What It Is, What It Isn't, and How to 'See' It, Even When It's Hidden

Although it's not considered a 'newly' diagnosed condition, BPD is relatively new to the field of research. It's been a puzzling condition to both differentiate from conditions with similar symptoms, as well as to be seen as a stand alone condition with its own diagnostic procedures, causes, treatment, and prognosis. Even part of the clinical term ('borderline') has been the platform of debate.

Initially, this condition was viewed as a 'borderline' between psychosis and neurosis, which wasn't really accurate. Plus, the term doesn't describe the condition well, leaving others to believe sufferers merely have a problem with their personality that can be tweaked, rather than a debilitating condition that interferes with a person's ability to function. That's the base of a great deal of misjudgment and prejudice leading society to forget that BPD is a clinical diagnosis, not a definition of the individual.

Today, there is more focus on a sufferer's inability to self-regulate, as well as their struggles with their emotions, cognitive thinking, behaviors, relationships, and self-image.

While learning about this confusing disorder, one way to look at it from the sufferer's point of view is by thinking of it as having nerve endings that are constantly exposed and vulnerable. That would make a person much more sensitive to everything, right? Being that sensitive would tend to make a person highly reactive, even if the trigger didn't seem major to the average viewer (that would equal an internal nuclear war to the sufferer). Not being able to shield those exposed nerve endings can result in the inability to calm down that leads to aggressiveness, inconsolable responses, and finding maladaptive, impulsive, or even dangerous, ways to adapt. *That* is the side of BPD that supporters, or people completely unaware of the condition, see.

A person going through these intense thoughts and emotions aren't even able to tell us what's going on inside of them because they aren't in touch enough with themselves enough to explain to others what's in their head. Their self-image, even what they like or don't, are confusing and questionable to them. They doubt everything and everyone, and trust? In simplest terms, they don't.

We'll go over nine of the most common signs in BPD sufferers. Each person living with this condition will experience different combinations of the following, and even at different levels of intensity, but for the most part these become obvious:

1. **Untrusting.** Individuals with BPD often misinterpret others' motives. They don't trust their own thoughts or motives, so when another person does or says something that isn't in line with their own line of thoughts, they often have feelings of suspicion. In worst case scenarios, they may even experience *dissociation* where they'll literally disconnect with their self-identity.

2. **Abandonment anxiety.** This is a significant sign and a very common trigger for many BPD sufferers. They fear being left alone or abandoned so much that something as small as not getting an immediate response from a text, or as impacting as a loved one being late coming home is enough to catapult them into a panicked state.

3. **Volcanic anger.** These individuals have explosive anger and short fuses. It doesn't take much to set them off. They'll yell, throw things, and seem inconsolable in their anger, but they rarely take it out on others. Most times, their anger is internal and stemming from their negative feelings toward themselves. And there are moments when their

anger comes fast, hard, and out of nowhere.

4. **Unhealthy relationships.** These individuals tend to gravitate to relationships that are intense, short-lived, and emphasize their insatiable feelings of unworthiness. They may even try believing what they feel is true love, only to be left with disappointment, and self-hatred. For them, relationships are either perfect or awful with no middle ground. This extends to friendships, family or other close relations where the other person often feels they're spinning just trying to understand what's expected of them.

5. **Emptiness.** This is one of the more heartbreaking, and hardest to understand, symptoms. These individuals have an unfillable hole, leaving them in a constant state of feeling like 'nothing' or life is 'meaningless.' They try filling this void with food, substances, sex, or other temporary satisfaction often making them feel even worse. From a loved one's view, it's so upsetting because it feels that all attempts of trying to make the sufferer happy in some way, nothing

seems to work.

6. **Uncertain self-image.** When a person doesn't connect with their inner self or identity, they can't be stable with their self-image. They can go from sky-high confidence (leaning to the side of arrogance), crashing to self-hatred—sometimes within a few minutes. This uncertainty about the self results in an unclear idea of who they are, or where they want their life to go. This causes them to change friends, jobs, lovers, ethics, values or even their sexuality.

7. **Harmful behavior.** Self-harm, impulsiveness, and behaviors that put the sufferer in risky situations is not unusual. From an outside view, this can be seen with shoplifting, eating disorders, risky sexual encounters, or substance abuse. Basically, anything the BPD sufferer does in this mindset is excessive and with no regard for personal safety.

8. **Self-harm.** We've pulled this one out as a separate point because the practice can be seen in most

cases of BPD. Although this group is high-risk for attempting suicide, self-harm is the act of hurting oneself without the intent of dying. It can be seen as cutting, burning, purging, choking oneself, etc. Even behaviors such as piercing or tattooing can be taken to this point.

9. **Mood swings.** This is one of the base components of this condition, and a main symptom shared with similar conditions (e.g., bipolar disorder). Extreme and unstable swings are in mood intense and happen often, but do tend taper off as quickly as they come on.

These are some of the main signs, but several of them are listed in other conditions. So in order to ensure that a correct diagnosis is given, there also needs to be a solid understanding of what BPD isn't.

What BPD Isn't

There are several frustrations both for those who love a person with BPD, and for those who are diagnosed with it. One is that there is no biological test that can distinguish one mental or psychological condition from another. Another is that BPD is one of the most misdiagnosed conditions. So much so that there's no accurate prevalence of the condition except an estimate that between 2% and 6% of the population have BPD (*NAMI*, 2017). If this is true, it shows prevalence warranting more research. So why, then, is this condition so highly misdiagnosed?

Here are a few possible reasons:

- **Misunderstanding about the base of BPD.** Not understanding the difference between *mood* disorders and *personality* disorders. The former category involves conditions where individuals display severe and rapid changes in mood. The latter involves conditions focusing on irregular ways of thinking, feeling, and behaving that are different from the social norm which results in distress and ability to function.

- **Social and professional stigmas.** There is a tremendous amount of stigma attached to a BPD diagnosis, not just with society but even among mental health professionals. In fact, this stigma can do more harm to individuals and their loved ones who just want answers. To make this point clearer, the base of stigma is judgement, blame, and discrimination. These are all worry points for a person who lives with BPD, making them feel even more ashamed leading them to try hiding their condition even more deeply. Repressing or hiding their condition leads to even more severe emotional dysregulation and attempts with dangerous ways of coping. Plus, there are many mental health professionals who won't diagnose a person with BPD as the label tends to stick with them throughout their lifetime.

- **BPD isn't treated as a whole condition.** As mentioned earlier, there are many other conditions that have the same symptoms as BPD, and a person with BPD can also have these conditions as part of their overall diagnosis. When professionals focus more on the individual conditions, rather than treating BPD as a whole condition, the sufferer may not be receiving the treatment specialized to their disorder.

- **BPD isn't gender-specific.** This is an important point. Women, by nature of their gender, are often highly misdiagnosed with mood-related disorders, while men are often undiagnosed. This should be a concern for those trying to get to the bottom of their or loved one's mental health issues. In these modern times, one's gender alone should not be a deciding factor in diagnosing BPD or any mood disorder.

- **BPD isn't age-specific.** There are many professionals who see BPD in youth, but hesitate in stamping a teen or young adult with such a heavy diagnosis. The concern is that the stigma of the disorder will follow the youth into adult life, resulting in being unfairly discriminated against. This hesitation prevents many youth from receiving proper treatment, which could prepare them better for coping with their condition down the road. The earlier it's detected, the higher the changes the youth has of becoming a productive adult.

There are many other factors that may interfere with

obtaining a proper diagnosis, and it's the lack of understanding that prevents many people from getting the help they need. The more families and loved ones of sufferers educate themselves with these issues, the better they'll be able to advocate for getting the right diagnosis and treatment.

Distinguishing Among the Four Types of BPD

In our next chapter, we'll be going through the diagnostic process for BPD. It may be valuable for those going with a loved one along this difficult road to be armed with information ahead of time. There will be a great deal of jargon, diagnostic terms, and other things that may not be easy to understand. The whole process may be easier to digest when the person being analyzed, as well as those by their side, have some knowledge behind them. Family members and loved ones need to remember that they know the sufferer better than anyone else, which makes them an expert and a valuable part of the treatment team.

There are four main categories of BPD, although an

individual can be set under more than one or different ones along their treatment journey. For the sake of our discussion, we'll separate them so that family members and/or loved ones can ask questions or raise concerns certain symptoms may not be known or seen.

1. **Impulsive.** The focus of those under this category is their impulsiveness, often expressed in dangerous ways. Their actions are often carried out with no regard for their personal safety, for the feelings of others and with no concern of consequences for their behavior. Those with this type of BPD are often charismatic, energetic, detached, flirtatious, and motivated by what they want. Their displayed behaviors may include:

   a. binging—eating, spending, hoarding

   b. risky/self-destructive actions—unprotected sex, multiple sex partners, consuming substances excessively, driving while impaired, befriending individuals actively participating in risky behavior, or gambling

   c. aggression—angry outbursts, physical fighting,

breaking/throwing/hitting things, or yelling fits

2. **Discouraged.** This is also termed "quiet BPD" because a lot of their symptoms are directed to themselves and hidden. They have an intense fear of being alone or being abandoned, often taking extreme measures to ensure they aren't. They keep their emotions deeply buried, and lay blame on themselves even if it's unwarranted. They are clingy, needy, codependent, and inconsolably moody when abandonment fears are triggered. Individuals in this category are also known to:

a. be perfectionists

b. feel detached in large groups

c. disbelieve they have strong connections with others

d. seek approval but also isolate

e. self-harm or experience continued suicidal thoughts

f. suffer feelings of continued loneliness or

emptiness

g. be successful or high-functioning

3. **Self-destructive.** Individuals in this category are consumed with self-hatred and bitterness. Those in this category display many symptoms similar to bipolar disorder. Symptoms such as restlessness, abnormally high energy level, feelings of euphoria, and decreased desire for sleep could be mistaken as mania, so loved ones need to be able to distinguish between mania and this form of BPD. Those in this category often display:

a. substance abuse—alcohol, recreational drugs, over-the-counter and prescription medications

b. risky, adrenaline-inducing behavior—the concern is less on the activity itself and more on the person jumping in impulsively without thinking

c. self-harm—cutting, burning, choking, scratching, hitting, pulling out hair, etc.

4. **Petulant.** Individuals in this category may seem angry one moment, then inconsolable the next. Their mood swings are huge, intense, and unpredictable. Those in this category believe they are unloved and unworthy, which leads to them having challenges in relationships. Their unhealthy need for control is fed by their manipulative nature, and they often resort to maladaptive ways of coping with their discomfort. Petulant sufferers can be seen as:

   a. irritable and impatient

   b. stubborn and defiant

   c. passive-aggressive

   d. having severe mood swings

Above all else, people within each of these categories experience a tremendous amount of emotional pain, which they may not even understand themselves. These different categories show how two people with BPD will experience the condition very differently, and one person can experience it in many different ways.

This may shed some light on how supporters may feel lost with their efforts in trying to help. Rest assured that even though the sufferer may seem different from one day to the next, or even one moment to the next, it's important to show ongoing and unconditional love and support in any scenario. It matters, even if they don't have the words to say so.

Things That People With BPD Want Us to Know

BPD is a scary condition to live with, and even scarier to watch. For those of us on the outside looking in, as hard as we try we can't possibly understand what's going on underneath. They push us away not because they don't want us there, but because they don't know how to make us see the world the way they do. And rather than allowing us in, they tell us to stop trying to help. Of course, we aren't just going to turn away.

In addition to arming ourselves with knowledge before venturing down that diagnosis and treatment road, it may also be helpful for supporters to bring how their loved one with BPD may be feeling. Here are a few insightful points, important to shed light on in an initial intervention meeting:

- **We're scared you'll leave us, even if things are okay.** Their deep-felt fear of abandonment is there even when a relationship seems to be going well. They're afraid they'll do something wrong, that they don't deserve us, and legitimately wonder why we stay by their side. This makes them seem 'needy' or 'clingy,' and it may be hard to deal with, but it stems from a real fear they have.

- **Life is emotionally painful, like living with untreated burns.** Imagine how difficult life could be if we had no control of our emotions or our responses. How difficult would it be to explain how we could be elated one moment, then minutes later be inconsolable and have no idea how we got there? *That* torment is how BPD feels, and they come across as 'over-sensitive' when they have no control over those things.

- **I feel everything to the extreme.** As touched on

earlier, there is no middle ground for those with BPD. You're either sky high, or lower than low, and there's no in between. This part of the condition is exhausting not only for them, but for every person around them. But in their mind it's 'normal,' and they are confused or even hurt when we react negatively.

- **I don't have multiple personalities.** This point is added in here to show why, sometimes, BPD is misdiagnosed. A person with this condition doesn't have more than one personality. They have a disorder that affects how they're able to regulate their emotions, thought patterns, and behavior, and may withdraw when feeling low, but this is not an indication of having other personalities.

- **I don't mean to be manipulative, and I'm not dangerous to you.** To clarify, not all BPD sufferers are manipulative or dangerous. When they are manipulative, it isn't with malicious intent. Most times it's to try convincing others they're doing better than we believe them to be.

And they are rarely dangerous to anyone. In fact, the only person they're in danger to is themselves.

- **Treatment is exhausting, disappointing, and frustrating.** We'll be going further into this point in a later chapter but, we need to be empathetic on this. We as supporters move with our loved one from one form of therapy or treatment to another, and don't always see the results we hope for. Think of how a person with BPD must feel in that situation? For an individual who already has little or no hope, trying one treatment after another with no real improvement can often make them feel they're 'unfixable.' One response to this that we'll go back to every so often in our discussions is: We don't 'fix' people; we help heal them.

- **I want so much to be loved, I just don't always know how to.** Individuals have so much love in them. So much so it can often feel smothering and overwhelming. Although it can be difficult to have a relationship with them, all they want is to know their feelings are returned, and that we won't leave them.

As you move forward into the diagnostic and therapeutic step, remember that by gaining a compassionate understanding perspective of BPD, and how it affects our loved one, you are doing everything you can.

And they know.

CHAPTER 2

The Diagnostic Process

Mental health problems don't define who you are.
They are something you experience. You walk in the
rain and you feel the rain, but, importantly, you are not
the rain.

–Matt Haig

Those of us who have tried the best we could to help our loved one through all the ups, downs, fits, rage, threats of harm and suicide get to a crossroads. One path confirms all we've been told from everyone around us who don't see this person the way we have. Those are the ones who tell us our struggling loved one is 'fine' and that they are just 'eccentric' or in a stage. Discounting what our gut has been telling us for a long time. The other path is the handful of people who confirm what our gut has been telling us. They know our loved one isn't 'fine,' 'eccentric,' or in a stage they'll grow out of. And that's the path we have to follow to get help. But it won't be an easy one.

Of course, there is the positive aspect of finally having a name for the unseen thing that has been controlling our loved one every waking moment. It's a relief to most supporters to have an explanation for everything their loved one has been through, and hope it will be the first step in getting effective treatment.

This chapter focuses on the diagnostic process from getting a referral all the up to figuring out the best form of treatment and/or therapy, and everything in between. It can be a long, frustrating, and turbulent time, especially if a loved one isn't able to get in to see an expert right away. We're also going to describe the process, including who will be on the mental health team. We'll also expand on points made in the last chapter on why BPD is difficult to distinguish from other conditions with similar symptoms, even though it's known to be treated for more than one mental health or psychological condition simultaneously.

Finally, we'll be closing the chapter with a special section on BPD in young people, and some more ways to view the condition through the eyes of the sufferer. We want to create the most complete picture of BPD possible because the more we understand the whole of who they are, the more trust they'll have in us to help them.

How BPD Is Diagnosed

When a person is physically ill, and is able to identify specific symptoms they can share with their primary healthcare provider, digging for the cause of the illness can be found relatively easily. There are many answers in our blood, for example, so a thorough series of bloodwork will enable the physician to follow a path to pin down the cause. For a person who has more internal illness concerns, the path isn't as clearly set.

There is no blood test that detects a mental or psychological concern, such as BPD. There are no scans, X-rays, ultrasounds, or any other sort of procedure that would help a doctor figure out what is causing an individual to think and behave the way they do. There may be certain MRI tests that can eliminate specific health issues, such as tumors, but that's a reach at best. This is a major concern for any of us wanting answers for our loved one, and why we feel anger and frustration with not knowing where to turn.

It can be a lengthy process because all there is to go from initially are the behavioral symptoms that can be seen, and the cognitive symptoms that are overtly coped with (e.g., self-harm). It's discouraging as a supporter or loved one to feel there's nothing that can be done until the affected person either reaches out to us, which rarely happens, or hurts themselves to the point of hospitalization. These shouldn't be our only options., which is why we'll share suggestions on how to maneuver through the right channels to get a loved one into the hands of the person who'll be able to help them.

Let's start with discussing the professional path who are the main players on the BPD diagnostic team:

- **Primary healthcare provider.** Whether this is a traditional doctor, naturopath or other sort of health professional, this is usually the person to get the ball rolling. Normally in order to see a mental health specialist, there needs to be a referral from the GP or family physician. This is based on symptom concerns or any sort of visible self-harm, or even if the person has a history of depression or anxiety. The problem is that it can be a long wait to see a specialist, and in many situations this isn't feasible. In these situations, it's wise to have a person who can see the sufferer until there's an opening with a specialist.

- **Psychologist.** There are many psychologists who work through clinics or physician's offices where a person can get immediate help while waiting to be seen by a psychiatrist. Supporters should make it clear with the physician that the psychologist should have experience working with individuals who have the exact symptoms the sufferer displays or, even better, a person who has direct experience working with individuals who have serious mental health concerns. It's important that the person with BPD feels safe and has a connection with who they'll be seeing, and that person should be available to see the sufferer regularly. Avoiding the possibility of feeding the individual's fear of abandonment needs to be in the open from the start.

- **Nutritionist.** This isn't always necessary but if the sufferer is practicing self-harm in the form of purging or other sort of eating disorder, this individual needs to be a part of the team. A brain that is nourished is in a healthier place to accept other forms of intervention that will happen.

- **Drug/alcohol counselor.** Again, not every individual with BPD will turn to substances to ease their symptoms but a large portion of them do. In that case, if the psychologist doesn't have specific experience in this area, it would be a good idea to have the physician recommend a person who's an expert in eliciting healthier ways of coping.

- **Psychiatrist.** It can take up to a year or longer to get in to see a psychiatrist, especially one who specializes in conditions such as BPD. This person would be considered the head of the team since they decide the procedures that can be tried as well as any sort of medicinal approaches that may ease symptoms. They have authority to prescribe medications and, usually, have access to a wider options of treatment than psychologists do.

In the case of younger individuals, other members of the mental health team might be school counselors as the connection to the person's needs in school, as well as a connection with Child and Family Services in the case of any family issues contributing to triggers.

After an assessment of the symptoms the person has— there need to be at least five out of the nine symptoms discussed in the first chapter—there are usually discussions with family to get a history as well as to get a full picture of what others close to the sufferer have noticed. The individual will also have to go into detail regarding their symptoms including which ones are most debilitating and how they interfere with everyday living. That may be the hardest part because those living with BPD aren't always able to express what they're feeling or have connections with what they're experiencing.

What can we do, as supporters, to make sure that the mental health team has everything they need to put together the best therapeutic plan? We know firsthand that a person with BPD isn't always upfront with what they're going through, nor will their trust issues allow them to be honest that they're struggling to others. Be rest assured that these experts know exactly what individuals with BPD will do, and they know what to watch for.

Here are a few common things that people with BPD will say or do when they need help, but don't come right out to say so. These can be added to the list brought to the mental health team, so they know what to expect when working with the sufferer:

- **I'm fine.** Most of us say these words when we don't want to talk. It's the fastest way to say, "I'm really not fine, but I don't want to talk about it right now." For a person with BPD, this can't be an acceptable response because when they aren't encouraged to talk about it, they're already past the point of being okay and moving into a total meltdown phase. Let the team know if this is a typical response and to leave it with that response.

- **I'm overwhelmed.** This isn't one that we'll hear many people say, especially younger sufferers, because admitting this means they aren't in control, or close to falling apart. But if they're brave enough to say so, immediate intervention is needed.

- **Maybe I'm supposed to be alone.** This is the all-or-nothing perspective leaking out. The usual tactic here is to be told that they aren't meant to be alone, and that they'll still have us. Remember that their abandonment fear comes across as them pushing us away, but it's almost like being tested that we won't leave.

- **I don't feel good.** This is a simpler way of saying that things are brewing inside of them and if they don't have a safe way of releasing it, they'll explode. Those who aren't as versed with BPD may think this is hinting at something more physically wrong, but it's much deeper than that.

- **I don't know.** When asked what's wrong, this is a very typical response. What's important to remember is that they have so many emotions and thoughts going on, they may truly not know what exactly is wrong. How can they explain to us what's wrong if they don't know themselves?

- **I'm sorry.** Those with BPD apologize often, even when they have nothing to apologize for. When we look at them closely, we'll see that they are literally terrified of everything: their feelings, disappointing us, being a burden, or even their own minds. They need to know they don't need to be sorry for what's happening inside of them, and we aren't going anywhere.

- **I'm going to bed.** Sometimes when the world is too much to handle, they think that the best thing for them is to shut the world out by going to sleep. What they really need is to be distracted from their thoughts. As supporters, we know that in that frame of mind leaving them alone with their thoughts is a dangerous thing.

- **I just have a headache.** Quite often, individuals with BPD will say this to us when we notice a change in their mood, when they aren't very responsive, or when they "space out." This is also an excuse to go lay down. It's a beginning sign that the person is struggling. Supporters should bring up to the mental health team if they ever noticed the sufferer asks for pain medication when indicating they have a headache. If the person practices self-harm regularly, it could be indicative of hiding pills for future use.

- **Do you want to hang out?** This is a way the person with BPD lets us subtly know they don't want to be alone. If they come to us every day, or a few times throughout the day, they're asking for help in their way.

- **I don't feel right/I feel weird.** This is a cry for help meaning that the person doesn't feel safe with their thoughts to the point that they're disassociating. The way their emotions or thoughts make their body respond feels strange and uncomfortable. They are asking not to be alone.

- **Saying 'okay' or giving a thumb's up.** Usually they do this not to worry those around them, when they don't have the energy or brain space to say more than that, or just to get us to back off a bit.

- **I've just been busy.** An individual with BPD doesn't want to let others know they've been avoiding social scenes, or isolating to not face others, so they lie. It's better, in their mind, to say they've been too busy to stay in touch rather than that they've intentionally been avoiding people.

- **I hate you/get out/leave me alone.** As hurtful as it is to hear these words, it's important that we remember that this isn't what our loved one wants to say. They really don't want us to leave, but they're riddled with guilt, shame, frustration, or whatever they may be feeling at that moment, and those are the words that come out rather than, "Can you just sit with me for a minute?"

Even though it's a great idea to share with the mental health team that the sufferer uses any of these phrases regularly, they've probably had a few of them fired their way too. Anything you share with the team, no matter how insignificant it may seem, is a step closer to creating the best possible therapeutic path for the sufferer.

Throughout the diagnosis process, remember that the team is careful when administering a BPD diagnosis because there are several other conditions that have similar symptoms, and in order for treatment to be as effective as possible the diagnosis must be accurate. A person can have other diagnoses with a BPD one (e.g., depression, anxiety, PTSD, etc.), but each is a separate condition that needs to be treated individually.

Things We Shouldn't Do With A Person with BPD

We've dealt with our loved one with BPD for awhile, and have tried helping them cope as best as we can. As soon as we are able to move our loved one onto the therapeutic path, we discover that some of the tactics we've tried, just to make things go a little more smoothly, may not have been the best strategies. The mental health team will guide you to tweak ones that worked, or to remove others that unintentionally accelerated the situation at hand.

Even experts in BPD will miss signs or clues because even though sufferers may not understand their condition, they do know how people respond to the things they say and do. Unfortunately, there's a lot of room for misunderstanding and miscommunication when being close to a person with this condition. It's hurtful to know we've been lied to, mistreated, or manipulated by the person we are simply trying to help. But we'd never just give up on them.

The mental health team is made up of people who are experts in the condition itself; family, friends, or loved ones are the experts in day-to-day life with the person affected by it. While waiting for our therapy plan, the top priority is to acknowledge that boundaries need to be set and stay firmly maintained. These boundaries help establish rules to avoid or distinguish confrontations, arguments, or misunderstandings more quickly. And they also help to prevent any maladaptive actions to be absorbed into routine, making it much more difficult to change.

That all being said, when establishing these boundaries, supporters should *not*:

- **feed into neediness for attention**. Not all individuals with BPD want or seek attention, but some do. It's usually seen as bringing in another person into an argument (e.g., *triangulation*), receiving validation for things they shouldn't be doing, or trying to get a rise out of us. The best way not to feed into this behavior is minimizing our own reactions, and not allowing others not directly involved in a situation to add to the chaos.

- **normalize behavior or minimize our intuition.** As human beings, we all experience intense emotions periodically that affect our behavior. We all get angry, and we've all had moments where we've overreacted. But when the behaviors are intense and happen often, the behavior needs to be addressed. When things seem truly wrong, they usually are, and normalizing or minimizing it won't help.

- **get pulled into the drama.** As an extension of the point on triangulation, we shouldn't allow ourselves to be drawn into the middle of a situation. To avoid this from happening, don't discuss a situation with anyone outside of the situation.

- **believe that they'll "get over it" or "snap out of it."** Those of us who've dealt with our loved one long enough already know these are not feasible thoughts. Individuals with BPD aren't able to just "snap out of" a mindset they get into because they don't have the tools to cope effectively yet. Don't be told, or allow others to think, this is a possibility.

- **normalize any sort of harmful or risky behavior.** This is a tough one because individuals with BPD aren't always candid with their behavior. For example, finding out that they didn't 'just go for coffee' with a friend, but were actually having a sexual encounter with a random partner. It may be difficult to accept that the sufferer in our life is engaging in high-risk behavior or seeking stimulation in ways that are unhealthy and dangerous. This will continue if their actions are normalized in any way.

- **be made to feel deeply hurt by impulsive remarks.** Many individuals with BPD struggle with deep anger management and impulsivity. Regardless of all they're going through, they shouldn't be allowed to disrespect or devalue those close to them. In such cases, the person needs to be called out for such treatment and have the boundaries re-established. If the treatment continues, supporters should distance themselves until the boundaries are respected again.

- **be drawn into the sufferer's abandonment fears.** A person with BPD has difficulty with making relationships work because they either push the individual away when they get too close to avoid any anxiety, or the sufferer bombards the person with needs for attention and companionship. One has to be careful with how they empathize with a person who has BPD who has these strong fears of abandonment. It's possible to be supportive without inadvertently enabling.

- **be emotional 'prey.'** This is difficult for a supporter to see clearly when their heartfelt intention is simply to be there. An example here would be the sufferer asking for money or to have things bought for them, then don't need the supporter after that. This is another area where those boundaries need to be set up.

- **allow undesirable behavior to become habitual or routine.** This point also falls in line with being emotionally guilted into agreeing to things that the sufferer will make routine. Some examples might be eating alone in their room (especially if they have an eating disorder), being on their device past the time or duration allowance, or going/staying out past curfew. Once an undesirable behavior becomes routine, it's much harder to have rules respected or to reset the boundary.

- **be the main 'go to' person all the time.** It's a wonderful feeling to be the one the BPD sufferer turns to when things are too much for them. But it also means that their 'go to' would also be the one they manipulate the most or treat the worst because, in their head, they know we'll stay no matter how negatively we're treated.

- **respond to their attempts at control or manipulation.** To respond emotionally to any sort of ill-treatment the sufferer attempts gives them leeway in believing they have control over us. The less we respond to their actions, the less likely they'll keep trying.

- **be manipulated into their harmful cycles.** This is also a tough point because we always want to be there. There are times that are triggers for the BPD sufferer such as Birthdays, holidays, summertime, etc. These are those times when they display symptoms, but they'll also try getting what they want from us using those painful times for them to get it. We need to be strong enough to call the person out, and remind them you're there to help them in ways you can but it isn't fair that they draw us into their pain cycle.

- **participate in codependency.** We absolutely want to help and to be a strong presence in their lives, but there's a fine line between being unconditionally supportive and empathetic, and being codependent. The former shows we're there for them, but will not allow them to be codependent. Even with a condition like BPD, the person needs to take accountability for their actions. We aren't responsible for their choices, they are.

With these points laid out, it's easier to see that even though we're by their side through their diagnosis and treatment path, we can still do more harm than good if we aren't in tune with the person and know when they truly need our help or when we're enabling them. Once in therapy, the mental health team can offer valuable strategies to make us aware of these attempts and the best way to ward them off.

BPD vs Bipolar Disorder

Ever since BPD was included in the Diagnostic and Statistical Manual of Mental Disorders (DSM-MD) in 1980, it's been the focus of controversy. The main reason for this is because there still hasn't been a resolution to whether or not it's related to bipolar disorder as the two disorders share so many similar symptoms. Although there are similarities, there are also different symptoms specific to each disorder that distinguish them as separate.

Similarities

The main reason there are experts who believe that BPD and bipolar disorder are related is because they both focus on mood instability and extreme impulsivity. Those with bipolar experience high mood swings between mania and depression. In a manic state, they have a decreased need for sleep and are active, often taking on many tasks at once. These severe changes in mood can last weeks or months at a time at each point.

Those with BPD also experience mood swings, emotional dysregulation, and instability. The moves from one extreme to the other can be within minutes at times, but don't last as long as what's seen in bipolar individuals.

Differences

With the similarities, there are major differences that separate the two disorders:

- The quality of the mood disorders differs. For bipolar individuals, the moods go from elated highs (mania) to extreme lows (depression). Those with BPD are in a constant state of emotional pain, feelings of emptiness, panic, anger, hopelessness, and loneliness.

- Changes in mood for those with BPD usually occur after an environmental trigger, where a person with bipolar's mood changes often seem to come from nowhere and not usually not triggered.

- Those with BPD rarely experience feelings of

elation. Normally, they go from feeling upset to 'okay.' Bipolar is either devastatingly low, or extremely elated.

There is continued research being done on BPD, but there hasn't been enough proven evidence so far that the two are related. It's important for supporters to make sure to advise the mental health team of any family history of either, or both, disorders so a more accurate diagnosis can be given.

The main concern is that because both of these conditions require medication, at least focusing on the mood regulation, a misdiagnosis would also mean incorrect administration of medications. For example, someone with bipolar needs to be treated for *both* mania and depression requiring specific medicinal regimen. For a person with BPD, there isn't a specific medication to treat it beyond antidepressants and mood regulators. Administering either condition with the wrong medications could have detrimental effects, so making sure the diagnosis is absolute is vital.

If nothing else, having this information may guide

supporters through the diagnosis with less turbulence. There will be days when what the mental health team tells us has question marks all over it. Sufferers should never be intimidated to ask questions, bring information of their own to the table, or even share any concerns regarding the diagnosed condition.

In the end, every person wants the same thing. We all want what's best for the sufferer, and for them to finally reach a level of happiness they deserve to feel.

CHAPTER 3

Treating a Person With BPD

I understand your pain. Trust me, I do. I've seen people go from the darkest moments in their lives to living a happy, fulfilling life. You can do it too. I believe in you. You are not a burden. You will never be a burden.

—Sophie Turner

The diagnostic process was difficult, but the positive that came from it was finally having a name for what's been plaguing your loved one. There's an explanation for their intense behavior, and now there's something to research further. Being aware of a condition fills us with hope that we can finally do something to help our loved one. Don't lose that hope, because it will help us move the individual forward no matter what hurdles pop up along the path to healing.

There are several options available for treating a person with BPD, and what works in one person's situation may not be helpful at all to another. That's why it's so important to work with the mental health team in finding the "right fit." It will take time to find the right treatment plan that helps to ease symptoms, rather than escalating them. This means trying different strategies, or the combination of several, until something clicks. It can be a difficult process for both the sufferer as well as those of us who just want the individual not to hurt anymore.

It's important for those supporting a loved one with BPD to keep two things in mind. First, the situation will seem worse before it gets better. It's similar to healing a wound that has been left untreated for too long, and has gotten infected. The infection has to be dealt with and cleared up before the wound can heal properly. This will be the most difficult part of the treatment process, but one that the individual has to go through so they can learn to self-regulate.

The second point is that individuals with BPD often

fight treatment. This stems from their belief that they "can't be fixed" or they "don't deserve to live." It's the mindset that has to be changed before any treatment can be successful. People with BPD don't want to hear that everything will be okay or that they just need to stick things out, especially since many sufferers aren't future oriented. As supporters, we need to teach the individual to be there with us in the present, in the 'now,' so that they can accept what needs to be done. There are things in the past that they'll need to address, but those things have no place in the present. And the future is something to work toward, not to worry about today. Those living with BPD can't make that distinction yet, but they'll be able to as they move through treatment.

That's what we'll discuss in this chapter First, supporters are going to need strategies of their own to help their loved one. We'll cover some suggestions on moving through the ups and downs that will come up. We also want to help supporters be an effective part of the mental health team, but also be able to read signs of a possible meltdown before it happens. This scenario is often called *splitting*, and we'll share ways to see them coming as well as suggestions on how to talk the individual through it before it goes past the point of return.

From there, we'll go over a few of the common therapy methods sought when treating a person with BPD. These methods not only help the individual learn to express themselves in better ways, but they'll also learn to connect thoughts with actions and find more effective ways of self-regulating. Finally, we'll end the chapter with a discussion for those supporters who find their loved one either fights treatment, or just refuses help. As we know, we can't force the individual to accept the treatment. However, there are strategies we can try to guide them down the path.

In the end, we all have the same end goal: to help our loved one find their path to inner peace. They'll get there.

Just never give up hope.

Treating BPD: Methods, Strategies, and Guidance

The mental health team will discuss different approaches in treating an individual with BPD. There is no one set path for every person. There are different aspects that are considered before trying anything such as how long the person has been living with it, the intensity of their symptoms, past history, if there are any other conditions in addition to BPD, and the individual's reception of help. Setting a plan is one thing, but getting the individual on board with their own treatment is another thing entirely.

Before going ahead with the treatment plan, it's important for supporters to prepare themselves for the journey ahead. After all, unless the individual has been hospitalized the mental health team won't always be there when things hit the fan. We know more than any other person how stressful it can be trying to help someone with BPD, or even to know how to respond in a specific situation.

In the case of younger individuals with BPD, or those who have made suicide attempts, hospitalization is the first point of treatment. This will be discussed in greater detail in a few minutes. For now, let's go over some strategies for supporters:

- **Learn about BPD.** We've already covered the importance of learning all you can about this condition. Not only does it help us understand more about the person who is afflicted by BPD, it also gives a more omniscient view of the person. Learning about something we don't fully understand is empowering, and we'll need that down the road when advocating for our loved one.

- **Emit confidence and respect.** There's a high association between surviving childhood trauma and BPD. Not every person who goes through trauma will develop the condition, but with such a huge relation it's important for those giving support for these individuals to bear in mind they'll need to earn their trust. They have a damaged sense of safety and control not only with themselves, but with everyone in their world. To truly help them, we need to ensure that their opinions, choices, and voice matters throughout their treatment options as well as life in general. Helping them build that confidence in themselves is how they'll learn to trust others.

- **Honesty.** Their trust issues also inflate their fear of abandonment. That means while supporting those with BPD, we need to be honest in all of our interactions with them. We need to do what we say we'll do, not to make promises we can't fulfill, and never tell them what we think they want to hear. The truth may not always be easy for them to hear, but in the end they'll appreciate being told what they *need* to know.

- **Manage conflict effectively.** Most of us know that life is never a smooth ride, and conflict is inevitable when each of us has different views, thoughts, and opinions. For a person with BPD, though, conflict means we're disappointed, angry, or wanting to end the relationship. We need to do our best to stay in that gray area they can't see, and assure them that just because we may not see eye-to-eye with them on something they've said or done, it will never change our feelings for them.

Focus on the behavior, not the person, so they learn that even though you don't agree with the way they behaved, you'll still be there.

- **Encouraging maintaining professional connections.** Individuals with BPD may not be receptive to therapy or professional intervention because they don't trust others, they don't believe what they're being told, and they certainly don't like being told they have to do things a different way than they're used to. But supporters should remind them that the therapists are there to give them help in ways that may be beyond our ability. We should help them to, at the very least, take what they believe is helpful from a certain source, knowing they can alter the plan as they change.

- **Remind them of their strengths.** In an upcoming discussion, we'll be sharing how to see the positives in BPD. For now, this individual is being bombarded at every turn with what's 'wrong' with them and how to intervene in every possible scenario. What they need to hear more of is what their strengths are. These abilities, strengths, and talents are reminders that there is more to them than this condition. These strengths can also be used as positive coping methods to turn to when things feel too much for them.

- **Have fun.** They're surrounded by illness, therapy, and treatment all of the time. They also need positivity and fun mixed in. Give them memories to embrace in darker times so they know their world isn't all about BPD. Make them laugh. Do activities they enjoy. Have a picnic, go for a walk, watch a good show or concert, or any other way to forget the roles of 'sufferer' and 'supporter' for just a little while. Help them create new, beautiful memories.

- **Take any hints of suicide seriously.** Those with BPD are more at risk of suicide than almost any other group. That means that any attempt, or even hint to it, must be taken seriously. They aren't doing such things for attention, and should never be ignored. The best way to handle it is to show concern for their safety, and let them know you'd be willing to stay with them until the feelings subside.

The other point is that supporters need to practice self-care. It's stressful and exhausting to care for another person, so we must take time for ourselves too. The individual with BPD is prone to think 'me time' would mean they're burdening us. This time to care for ourselves isn't rejection or avoidance. After all, if we allow ourselves to go empty and not reenergize, how can we expect to deal with the bigger issues that come up when there's nothing left to get us through?

It makes everything else we face throughout the treatment process easier to cope with.

What Are the Common Treatments for BPD?

Usually the treatments for BPD involve psychotherapy, medication, hospitalization, or a combination of these. There are also further therapeutic methods that involve loved ones or family members so that there's full support for the sufferer. Here's a look into these areas:

- **Psychotherapy**. This is the typical form of

therapy in treating BPD, and is included in conjunction with the other forms of treatment. The mental health team may opt for one of the following:

- ○ Cognitive Behavioral Therapy (CBT): The focus of this therapy is to help individuals recognize unhealthy behavior, beliefs, or perceptions of the self and of others. It also teaches more effective ways to respond to aggressive, negative, or suicidal thoughts.

- ○ Dialectical Behavioral Therapy (DBT): The focus of this form of therapy helps individuals learn to recognize, be aware of, and deal with their beliefs and behaviors. It also helps people to interpret and respond more appropriately to other people's behaviors.

- ○ Schema-focused therapy: In a nutshell, the focus is helping people have a more positive view of themselves and the world around them.

- • **Medication.** As discussed previously, there is no medication that cures BPD, but the psychiatrist on the team may prescribe medications for mood, anxiety, and/or depression to ease symptoms. Medication is used in conjunction with therapeutic methods, which can be highly successful. The downside is that some individuals experience uncomfortable side effects that can enhance, rather than calm, the symptoms they're given to relieve. The person is unusually monitored closely in order to find the medicinal/therapeutic that is most effective.

- **Hospitalization.** This is usually the starting point for some sufferers, and the last resort for others. Hospitalization is usually the path followed when there are concerns about suicide, or if there have been suicide attempts. Hospitalization is turned to as the 'stabilization' resort as the person is monitored until the right treatment path is found. There is concern with keeping people in the hospital too long, however, as the person isn't learning to cope in the real world when living in the protective atmosphere of the hospital.

Family-based therapy is available to loved ones of those

being treated for BPD where they can have therapy for themselves, or join sessions with the sufferer. These give ways for all people involved in the care and support of the individual to be on the same page, and to have any questions or concerns addressed. There are programs available to youth and teens diagnosed with BPD, which vary according to their age and what is available in their communities. Finally, holistic and alternative approaches can be highly effective for those living with BPD, which we'll go into greater detail in a later chapter.

What Is 'Splitting,' and How Do I Help a Sufferer Through It?

For those supporting a person with BPD, 'splitting' is an element of the disorder that is vital to watch for. It's essentially the cry of help before things hit the fan, and there are specific signs that may have been missed, but will be easier to pick up on the further we go down the therapeutic path.

It's when the sufferer only sees people or situations as good or bad, all or nothing, and stays in that gray area we discussed earlier. Not every person with BPD 'splits,' but it is usually a trigger response to rejection, abandonment, or reminders of childhood trauma (e.g., anniversary of events). The person goes into defense mode in order to avoid the uncomfortable, painful, or anxiety-ridden emotions connected with those situations or people. The following are some signs of splitting:

- **Saying hurtful things.** Lashing out to those of us closest to the sufferer is their way of getting rid of the feelings without actually having to deal with them. It's also a way to keep us at arm's length when they feel we're getting too close for comfort. There is usually a lot of guilt involved because they don't mean to hurt us, they just don't feel safe owning the feelings themselves.

- **Jumping to conclusions.** This is when the fear of abandonment kicks in causing them to assume the worst when there may be a logical, and opposite, reason. For example, the person texts or calls a close friend who doesn't respond all day. Their trigger reaction is to assume the person is avoiding them, or doesn't want to speak to them, when the person may just be busy. This is a common trigger and doesn't take much for them to reach this point.

- **Emotionally detaching.** This is seen as being cold, distant, and avoiding all methods of communication. Most times, they do this to avoid saying something they'll regret, but others it's simply a defense mechanism.

- **'Ghosting.'** We all have done this at some point, but a person with BPD does it from a different mindset and with a different purpose. This is their way of pushing someone away that's either a trigger for them, or a person they don't want to hurt if/when things get too much for them. It's another way to put their walls securely up.

- **Becoming highly irritable.** They have little patience, are quick to anger, and very thin-skinned. Those trying the hardest to support them will be the most likely to be on the receiver's end of this behavior. It could get to the point that even just checking in on them will be enough for them to scream at us to leave them alone.

- **Explosive anger.** This is a terrifying behavior to the brunt of, but they are more likely to take things out on inanimate objects or themselves than other people. It doesn't even take much to set them off, but it can be seen as yelling, purposely breaking things, throwing things, ripping things apart, hitting objects, or resorting to self-harm. This is one of the top behaviors to watch as closely as possible because they don't have enough self-control to stop themselves from causing damage, or seriously injuring themselves.

- **Canceling plans.** Quite often, this reaction happens in situations, or with people, where they feel they have to pretend to be okay. Whether it's at a family gathering or a friend's birthday party, it can be too exhausting to put a happy mask on, and keep it on, when they don't feel it. Canceling set plans is easier than having to force themselves to be someone they believe they have to be.

- **Isolating.** For many of us supporters, this can be a disconcerting response because we fear what they'll do when we let them be. In one way, it can be seen as a good thing because they know they're hurting and don't want to hurt anyone. Being alone is easier than taking things out on others. On the other hand, leaving a person with BPD alone with their thoughts gives them license to deal with stuff in harmful ways. If they ever want to isolate, let them. But we should check on them often, so they know we're just a shout away.

Some of these tactics may be all too familiar, but these are the most common signs that the sufferer is splitting. Know that these are a few steps before they take action on those displayed feelings. These are the times we try working them through those tough emotions in healthier ways. Sometimes they may want us to be right there, but not say anything. Other times they may want us to remove ourselves and let them sleep. Either way, we always need to let them know we're there whenever they need us.

In the next chapter, we'll be focusing entirely on the

glories and tribulations of loving a person with BPD. Even though we constantly feel we're being tested, pushed away, or an emotional punching bag, we love them with all of our heart. And beneath it all, they love and appreciate us, too.

CHAPTER 4

Loving Someone with BPD

Too often we underestimate the power of a touch, a smile, a kind word, a listening ear, an honest compliment, or the smallest act of caring, all of which have the potential to turn a life around.

–Leo Buscaglia

As we go through the diagnosis and treatment plan processes with our loved one, it can be truly heartbreaking watching them be seen as a "BPD patient" rather than an individual learning how to cope with that one part of who they are. Somewhere along the journey, the members on the mental health team are all about medication, symptoms, and therapy and overlook who's underneath all of that: a whole person.

No matter if it's a best friend, a child, a parent, a sibling, or any other family member or acquaintance, it's a helpless feeling when you don't know how to most effectively help a person who doesn't even seem like they want you to be near them a majority of the time. But with a team that is behind us, and our loved one following a new path, we shouldn't feel powerless anymore. They are fighting something they can't see, but feel with overwhelming intensity, every single day. Following their lead, we should continue with our unconditional support. There are a few things we're going to discuss in this chapter.

First, we're going to cover a few things about helping a loved one with BPD. This isn't just about understanding their condition, or knowing how to respond effectively to behaviors, it also means hearing what they try telling us about what's going on inside of them. We also need to know how to handle the scenario when a person with BPD avoids, or outwardly refuses professional help. There's much more involved than simply telling them it's best for them, plus we don't really know what fears they may have about accepting help. We'll offer some suggestions to gently nudge them to keep going.

Finally, we're going to cover two other points. The first is that it may be helpful, both for supporters and sufferers alike, to look at some of the good traits those with BPD have. It may be a surprise for the sufferer especially that there are actually positive things hidden away among the symptoms. The second point is one many supporters are reminded of, but rarely follow suit. We're going to review the importance of practicing good self-care. How can we expect to be there for our loved one when we are already running on empty? You'll have a few suggestions on taking precious time for yourself and how it helps everyone else.

Think of this chapter as the stepping-stone for advocating for a loved one when they're strong enough to get back to living their lives as an effective part of their community. That's the end goal for every person on the mental health team.

Supporting a Loved One Through Stormy Times

We know that communication is one of the main

components of any relationship. Those of us supporting a person with BPD, however, know that this is challenging on the best days. It isn't just because they don't understand what's going on inside of themselves enough to talk to us about it, there's also the feeling that anything we say can be taken completely out of context and inadvertently trigger negative thoughts.

Conversations with sufferers can be compared with having a heated discussion with a child. Sufferers often have trouble understanding nonverbal cues, and very often misread them. Our body language, the tone of our voice, even certain facial expressions can be taken the wrong way, causing them to respond aggressively and defensively. The disorder distorts the way they interpret messages, as well as what they want to say. It raises their frustration to a point where they shut down completely, and that's what we want to prevent.

They need to be truly listened to and have their feelings acknowledged, even if we don't always understand them. When we offer them that respect, and we learn how to alter how we communicate and respond to them, it does help to diminish the angry responses or meltdowns. It also helps to pick up on the best time to begin any sort of interaction with the sufferer. If they're already in an escalated state, it's not the best time to attempt a heart-to-heart chat. When things calm down, here are a few tips in practicing effective communication:

- **Listen actively and with genuine sympathy.** Active listening means giving the person 100% attention, with no distractions. No TV, no cell phones, and no devices. Those with BPD need to know they're being heard, which means to allow them to share whatever they need to with no judgment, opinions, or criticism.

- **Focus should be on feelings, not the words.** We know that individuals with BPD are telling us more than what their words say. Encourage them to just say whatever is on their mind with no worry about how it may sound coming out. Of course there are some lines not to cross over, such as being crude or inappropriate, but they should feel free to speak openly.

- **Stay calm, even if they're lashing out.** It can be difficult not to defend ourselves when they criticize or throw accusations our way, but it's important not to lose it. Losing our cool will only escalate the situation and that won't help either side.

- **If emotions rise, try using distraction tactics.** The best distraction strategies also calm and comfort. Some suggestions could be going for a walk, doing a short work out, having tea, love up the family pet, or do some cooking/baking. Distract using things they either like to do, or are good at.

- **Talk about things outside of their condition.** They get enough about their BPD through therapy, and may begin to define themselves through their condition. Even talking about 'fluff' stuff is a great way to keep communication open.

With the communication up and running, it's important that boundaries are also set. This isn't about helping the sufferer learn to create their own boundaries, it's equally as important for supporters to establish and strengthen theirs. When all boundaries are known and respected, it helps to develop trust among everyone which is the base of all healthy relationships. This is a valuable thing for those with BPD to work on.

Setting, maintaining, and strengthening boundaries is something the sufferer may not be happy with initially. This stems from their intense fear of abandonment and rejection, but we have to persevere because when we cave to their reaction we're basically rewarding poor behavior. But if we remain strong, it empowers all involved and leads to a better, trusting, respectful relationship.

A few 'do's and 'don'ts' to bear in mind include:

- **Do:**

  - assure the person that the boundaries are being set for the good of the relationship for *both* of you. Remind them that these things are what will make the relationship run more smoothly when we know what works and what doesn't on both sides.

○ have everyone on the same page with the same boundaries. It's also important to have understood consequences when they aren't respected.

○ introduce boundaries as the opportunity represents itself, rather than giving the whole list of boundaries in one shot. They'll be easier to digest, taken more positively, and receive less static.

● **Don't:**

○ make ultimatums right off the bat. Those never go off well. Boundaries will be tested to ensure that consequences will kick in when they're crossed. It's human nature. If the behavior continues even with the looming consequences that fall into place when they aren't respected, giving an ultimatum can be used as a last resort.

○ ever allow abusive behavior. State clearly that you wouldn't do that to them, so you will not tolerate it toward you.

o enable them. There is a strong difference between *helping* a person, and *enabling* them. When we're trying to help, it means the person needs a bit of assistance to get them past a hump but will be okay with the right tools if that happens again. On the other hand, to enable a person means we take away the accountability away from the person and take it on ourselves. This doesn't help the person learn to stand on their own two feet.

Once communication tactics and boundaries are in place, there are a few other ways we can help the sufferer while protecting ourselves at the same time. These suggestions are extras to keep close on days when we aren't feeling we're getting anywhere no matter what strategies we've tried on our own, or have been guided to through the mental health team:

• When set boundaries aren't being respected, resorting to gentle verbal guidance may be required. It could even be something worded as, "You need to speak calmly and respectfully to me if you want to continue with this conversation. If you aren't able to right now, we'll have to try again later once you're less angry."

- Bring the support team together on how to set boundaries that are in unison. In this way, the sufferer will soon realize that they can't single out one person they believe will take their abusive behavior and agree as a group how to handle situations when they arise.

- Supporters absolutely need a self-care plan, including time to themselves every day. It takes a great deal of patience, energy, and brain power to be by a sufferer's side. We need to take that time to recharge. There will be more on this point later on in the chapter.

- Most importantly, hurtful treatment is harmful to both the sufferer and to us down the road. So don't allow it under any circumstances.

Self-Care When Supporting a Loved One with BPD

As supporters of a loved one with BPD, it's natural for

us to make that person our number one priority. It's an admirable job without a doubt, but it's also draining, exhausting, and takes away from our overall health. By no means is this the sufferer's fault. We need to remind ourselves the importance of caring for us, so we have the energy to care for them. And that's what self-care is all about.

Many of us feel guilty even thinking about taking time away from the sufferer. But if we can come back refreshed, full of energy, and have a positive mindset, it's good for them, too. Here are vital ways to make sure we're on top of caring for ourselves when supporting our loved one:

- **Join BPD support groups.** This may not seem like self-care, but it is. By reaching out to others who truly understand the ins and outs of what it's like to help and support a person with BPD is good for the heart and soul. There is nothing less lonely than thinking you're the only one out there in the same boat. Reach out and you'd be surprised who reaches back.

- **Be around other people.** 'Self-care' doesn't necessarily mean alone time (although, that's important too). When your entire day, and most of the night, focuses on caring for another person, we need to avoid the lure of isolating ourselves. Of course, there are tons of creative things to do that don't require being around others, but socializing is healthy. Check in with friends, family or others who have nothing to do with illness, therapy, or treatments. Step away from it all for just a little while.

- **Manage stress.** When another person's anxiety, worries, and stress are at the forefront, our own stressors are often pushed on the backburner. But as we remind our sufferer, not facing things can build up to the point our overall health is impaired. Deal with stress effectively, and if it can't be, be sure to seek professional insight.

- **You're allowed to have fun!** As an extension of the first point, we often feel guilty about going out and simply enjoying ourselves. Or maybe we've forgotten how. We're allowed to go out to a movie, go window shopping, have lunch with someone we haven't seen in a while, or just go to the park for a nature walk.

- **Pay attention to physical health.** It's easy to ignore an ache, pain, or some other physical symptom that our health is being ignored. We need to make sure we're eating properly, keeping substance consumption to a minimum, getting enough sleep, and doing an activity to get the body moving. We also need to pay attention to things that may be out of whack. We all know that little aches and pains can turn into something more worrisome when we're not paying close enough attention.

Self-care is vital to everyone on the BPD support team. We need to make sure that our mind, body, and spirit are in sync, and securely connected. The best way to remember it is by remembering the "Three C's": I didn't *cause* it. I can't *cure* it. I can't *control* it. That's an empowering expression that we could write down, and pin up where our sufferer can say it too.

Yes, There Are Positive Traits of BPD

It may surprise many supporters to see the positives in our loved one living with BPD. When we focus on all of the symptoms and negatives of the disorder, we tend to forget that this is a *whole* person, and that BPD is only a part of their whole self. And it doesn't help when society still puts tremendous stigma on mental health struggles.

Many people who have BPD are highly intellectual, intelligent, and highly empathetic individuals. This section isn't to 'glorify' mental health issues or diminish its seriousness. We just want others to view sufferers beyond their diagnosis, so they don't become defined by it.

The following are positive traits of BPD, and we should remind sufferers of every single day:

1. **Deep empathy.** As touched on above, individuals are so emotionally connected with others that they've been known to take their emotions, pain, stress, or other feelings as their own. Perhaps others feel drawn to them because

they believe the sufferer will understand them at a level no one else will.

2. **Extremely resilient.** They probably can't even see this in themselves, but resilience is the trait of literally being knocked down, and having the strength and courage to get back up. Even though they see things in a black-and-white mindset, seeing self-harm as a release and suicide as a resolution, most times they stick it out and keep trying. That's powerful.

3. **Highly perceptive.** Even though in the throes of emotional meltdown, they often misinterpret what others say or do, they are more perceptive than we think. They're always watching, reading, and picking up on our vibes, and others may feel overwhelmed by the sufferer's ability to pick up on things the rest of us often miss.

4. **They see beauty in ways others don't.** Don't be mistaken. They may see themselves as unworthy or even unlovable in their lowest times, but have

an uncanny way of seeing the beauty around them in ways few others can.

5. **They understand invisible trauma.** As is the case with many mental health or psychological conditions, BPD is invisible. Others can't see the suffering, pain, or injury that's been inflicted upon them, or how deeply it's affected them. This knowledge and insight also plays a part in their compassion. They'd be superior in positions of advocacy where they are a voice for those who don't have one.

6. **Deep capacity for love.** As we've learned in earlier discussions, BPD sufferers may not have positive personal images, or falsely believe they're unworthy of love, but they love deeply. Their fears often stand in the way of expressing their capacity for love, but those who are able to get past those barriers will feel a pure form of love that may be overwhelming at first. Their love and loyalty extends to friends, family, and partners in life that they've allowed to get close.

7. **They express their pain artistically.** This is an amazing talent. Even when they don't have the words to express their deep level of pain, they can *show* it through music, art, poetry, or other forms of writing. Not only are the arts an empowering way to turn to more effective ways of coping, but their art may touch another person who needs that understanding.

There are probably other positive traits we can list, or the sufferer can contribute themselves. They hear enough about the negatives of their condition, and all the harmful ways they think and behave. Take time to remind them of all of the pluses they have, and they're more important.

This leads us to the next chapter where we learn how the condition not only affects sufferers and what we want outsiders to understand, we'll also share the most important aspects of BPD that the sufferers want others to know. These discussions are what will lead us to be strong advocates for our loved one.

CHAPTER 5

Healing Together

Being deeply loved by someone gives you strength,
while loving someone deeply gives you courage.

–Lao Tzu

This chapter's focus is on healing together as supporters and sufferers moving forward after the treatment plan has been set. There may be times where tweaks to the plan may be required as life ebbs and flows, but the base routine has been established. Now we need to find the best way to advocate for our loved one, so they learn how to advocate for themselves. This is an essential part of the whole process as the individual goes out to be a productive contributor to their community with as little stigma attached to them as possible. They deserve that, and it means eliciting greater understanding from all possible angles on BPD, and what it's truly like to live with it. After all, people only fear what they don't understand. Our goal is to change that.

We'll start with sharing facts others need to know about this condition from the mind of people who live with it every day. Remember that BPD is an invisible disorder, so the first step is helping others see it as a *part* of an individual, rather than a "BPD person." There's a difference.

From there, we want others to know about and understand what it looks like to close friends and families who are supporting a person with BPD. The reason the condition can be so difficult to pin down and diagnose is that the person becomes so good at keeping their symptoms under the radar, people outside of the sufferer's "inner circle" miss what's really going on. We'll be sharing facts every person should know about this disorder so we can all advocate most effectively.

We're then going to have an in-depth discussion focusing on how we can continue to effectively give on-going support to our loved one. Even though their mental health team may not be right there as part of the daily activities, as we are, they'll still need reminders, so their confidence remains high with functioning to the best of their abilities.

Our last discussion for this chapter will be focusing on suggestions for coping skills. These are ways to empower our loved one to take control of all they learned in therapy, and put them into play when their symptoms are triggered so they don't become escalated. These coping skills can be the stepping-stones for learning the mindfulness mindset, and living life holistically which we'll be focusing on in the final chapter.

For now, let's talk about ways to inspire our loved one to break the barriers of stigma and misunderstanding.

Open Minds, Inspire Acceptance, and Stop the Stigma

If all of us were willing to see the world through the eyes

of a person struggling with mental health struggles, even just for a short while, it would change the world's view of mental health dramatically. That means not just reading up on a condition, watching a show about it, or even hearing professionals talk about it. None of those views can give an outsider a true understanding of what the conditions are *really* like because they don't live with those conditions.

Many sufferers get to a point where they want to give up, not because of the condition itself but more because those who say they want to help are only adding to the chaos. They don't want to be talked over or talked about like they aren't even there when the professionals are talking about what they think is best for the sufferer. They don't just want to be treated symptomatically, and the core of their mental break is being ignored. And they get tired of not having their true needs acknowledged or met by those who are supposed to be helping them. Isn't their opinion, and the respect for their input equally as important? It should be.

They want to feel better after coming out of a hospital or treatment setting, not worse than when they went in.

That being said, these are some important points they want others to see and understand:

- **BPD is sometimes linked with other conditions.** We've touched on this point earlier, but from the sufferer's perspective it's important. The NIMH estimates that 1.4% of the population have BPD, and most of these people have comorbid disorders (*Personality Disorders*, 2022). There is no prescription to 'fix' or 'treat' BPD, but there are medications for specific symptoms relating to anxiety, depression, and mood regulation. The problem is that each person experiences the condition differently, and any prescriptions will also affect them differently. Some muffle some symptoms, but will elevate others at the same time. It can be a tiring, frustrating, and endless process trying to find the best medication regimen. Also, the symptoms from the other conditions the sufferer may have will affect their BPD too. Each person will have their own "BPD toolkit," where they'll have a plan made just for them and ways of coping with their symptoms.

- **The earlier BPD is detected, the better my chances are of learning to cope.** Youth and teens as young as 12 years old have been diagnosed with BPD, but there is great caution with stamping a young person with the label. It can be seen as a 'phase' young people all go through, so they need to be analyzed very carefully. But as with any sort of mental, psychological, or physical conditions are diagnosed, the earlier intervention can be made to set the person up for higher success.

- **A BPD diagnosis doesn't make me a bad person.** This is a mindset that sufferers often fall into. They convince themselves that because they handle things much differently than others, they're 'bad' or a burden on those trying to care for them. This is false and, in fact, having such a condition makes them insightful, compassionate, and the best possible spokesperson for others going through it.

- **Having BPD doesn't mean I'm a drama-seeker.** Those with this condition would love to be able to have a handle on their own emotions, and certainly don't revel in the attention they inadvertently get from meltdowns or breakdowns. It may seem as though they desire the attention because they often seek validation and acceptance, but they certainly don't want preferential treatment. It's often misunderstood.

- **BPD makes me feel unlovable.** Because they feel so much all at once, or absolutely nothing depending on the situation, an individual with BPD isn't able to express their true feelings in a proper way. As with any other situation in their lives, they are either intense in a relationship, or completely removed from it. This makes having a real relationship with them so difficult. This is where their belief that they're unlovable comes from, and they tend to push away to avoid either getting hurt or hurting someone they care about.

- **BPD interferes with my ability to have control over my emotions and responses.** An example to show this would be forgetting a Birthday. For most of us, this wouldn't be a huge deal. We'd send belated wishes and that'd be it. Life sometimes gets so busy these things happen. For a person with BPD, the same situation would be felt at a much deeper level. They'd feel guilty for forgetting, beat themselves up unnecessarily for not being there, and not forgive themselves. This could lead to other spurts of emotional responses, but this gives a visual. We'd consider this a four or five on the emotional scale and easily rectifiable, whereas the person with BPD would shoot this over ten. It's important for outsiders to remember that these are aspects of BPD the person is learning to keep in check and to have patience if it happens.

- **There's a link between BPD and trauma.** This isn't true in every case, but there are many BPD sufferers who have trauma in their pasts. When unresolved trauma exists, the emotional and mood dysregulation seen today has a direct connection with a situation from the past where they were felt initially. That trauma needs to be dealt with first in order to pave the way for success in treatment for BPD. Those who want to understand a person with BPD and their reactions need to bear in mind that trauma may be the stem of a portion of those reactions.

Those who aren't familiar with BPD may benefit from knowing how isolating and lonely the condition can be. With the constant fear of not knowing what out there will trigger something inside of them, they often choose not to go out at all. We can help them with those confusing feelings by building up their sense of self and the belief they are an important contributor to our world.

Self-Care Suggestions for Those Living With BPD

Self-care is a group of life skills to ensure we're taking care of ourselves as best as we can. We're going to focus on mindfulness in the next chapter but for this section, we want to cover self-care tips our loved ones should keep close when they face triggers or stressors in their environment.

- **When I feel overwhelmed:** It's suggested to

remind our loved one that when we focus on a situation one thing at a time, or one emotion at a time, it doesn't seem so big. Have the person breathe through the initial moment, then break the situation down into tiny, easier to deal with bits.

- **When I feel angry, frustrated, or restless:** This greatly depends on the sensory tolerance of the individual, but some tips can be ripping up paper or a plastic bag, punching a pillow, throwing a frustration foam brick, holding ice, 10 minutes of intense exercise, or doing outside chores. The idea is to distract from the initial discomfort of the emotion and to avoid trigger responses.

- **When I feel sad or alone:** This is one that depends on the person's age, as well as their tolerance for touch or other sensory input. Some options can be wrapping up in a blanket and watching a show; writing down negative thoughts, then ripping it up; listen to music that inspires or uplifts; writing a letter of comfort, or a journal entry, to the part that is sad or depressed; or cuddling a stuffed animal or pet. The key here is not only to distract from the negative emotion, but divert attention to a healthier way of coping with them.

- **When I am having a panic attack or feel stressed:** This involves methods that give comfort, and bring the person down from explosive to calm. Some ideas could be to have a favorite drink while paying close attention to the sensory input (e.g., flavor, temperature, feel of the glass); take in deep, deliberate breaths; be aware of everything around in that moment; or indulging in a hot bath or shower. The point with these suggestions is to have the person become one with how the panic or stress makes their body feel, then turn to specific ways that ease those unpleasant feelings.

- **When I "space out":** The focus would be keeping the person there in the moment and not to separate themselves from it. Some suggestions could be chewing something pungent like ginger or hot spices; clapping hands or tapping on the thighs until they can feel the sting; or drink ice water and chew on the cubes. One thing to be wary of here is not to allow the person to hurt themselves to feel/not feel. The clapping, for example, should stop once they've "woken themselves up" and not go any further.

- **When I want to harm myself:** We may have an idea if thoughts are going on to move the person this way, but we don't always catch them before they act on their thoughts. When they show signs of moving to self-harm, some things to try could include rubbing ice on the spot they want to harm; put a piece of tape on the skin, then peel it off; practice yoga or other form of meditation; or take a cold bath or shower. Again, the idea is to interrupt the thought/act line of thinking. We shouldn't do anything that feeds into the self-harm mindset but, rather, distracts from taking action.

Because our loved one can be so impulsive, these are great tools and strategies they can turn to in those fleeting moments. But what can they do in the long run, or when there isn't someone right there during those moments to remind them ways to distract themselves? Our hope is that they'll develop their own coping tools and turn to them when they need them. Until then, we can set them up by suggesting the following they can add to what they're already doing:

- talk to a trusted person whenever feelings start rising too quickly to control

- keep a mood diary where they can release all of their good and bad feelings and they're stored somewhere safe outside of themself

- plan ahead for stressful or difficult times by ensuring coping tools are in place, and that they have an effective counteractive way to deal with negative thoughts, emotions, or stressors

- create a "self-care box" where they can store all of the little things they find comfort from such as pictures of loved ones, scented candles, crystals, favorite CDs, book, or a fidget tool

- take care of physical health by ensuring healthy

eating, restful sleep, exercise, enjoying nature, and avoiding all forms of alcohol or drugs

- seek out professional resources to cope with any sort of bullying or maltreatment in the community

One of the main struggles in dealing with BPD is the discrimination our loved one endures in their community. It's the main reason they won't accept or seek help, even from those of us who try being by their side regardless of the situation. The next section touches on how to lovingly deal when this happens.

When Your Loved One Resists Help for Treating or Coping With BPD

It can be excruciating as a supporter when our loved one pushes us away, and keeps us at an arm's length, no matter how hard we try offering our help. We know we can't force them to willingly accept treatment, even if the person is a youth. The control for embracing the benefits of therapy is out of our hands, but our hearts won't give up even if they give up on themselves.

During times when they resist their therapy or

treatment, or "go along with it" so we and/or their mental health team will back off, we can still offer our unconditional support. Here are a few things we can try:

- **Encourage them to give treatment a try.** If we're willing to do anything possible to help our loved one, we fully support giving it a try. It may not seem to help initially, or might even seem overwhelming, but trying is better than doing nothing, right? That's the mindset we need to inspire in our loved one. They are leery about venturing into new situations more than most others are, but we need to work them through any anxiety or jaded beliefs they may have to test the waters before deciding it doesn't work.

- **Help them to understand their treatment.** We are already aware that BPD isn't easy to treat, but it's possible. If we learn all we can about the treatment to be tried on our loved one, we should become as versed with it as we can including any lingo and the process in general. What would also be helpful is if our loved one had ways they could practice their skills they're learning in therapy on their own. It gives them some power they feel they've lost, which will inspire them to keep facing forward.

- **Remind them how much we appreciate them.** Quite often, our loved ones will work really hard to make us happy. They do this to make up for any of their negative behaviors and to assure themselves that they haven't disappointed us to the point where we'd give up. The downside to this is that if we inadvertently don't acknowledge their efforts, they may take this to heart which starts the cycle all over again. They crave honest appreciation, validation, and our love so give it to them unconditionally whenever they're making their best effort.

- **Let them know that their mixed messages won't make you leave them.** They bounce back and forth between expressing their undying devotion to us, then turn around and hate us the next minute. As upsetting as this can be, they need to know that we'll be there through the times of fun and love, as well as the down and out times.

They're still the same person either way, and our love for them won't disappear.

- **Be as responsive as we can be.** If the loved one reaches out to us, we should respond as best as we can. This doesn't mean that we should condone being available on call at every moment of the day and night. Their go-to when they don't feel heard is to self-harm, but if we respond how we can when we can, it can diminish those trigger maladaptive coping tools.

- **It's not their fault.** We've said this a few times throughout previous chapters, but it's a good reminder. No matter how outrageous or extreme their reactions and behaviors are, they can't control them. They have a mental health issue with active symptoms, and that's how we should see it. They aren't doing, saying, or behaving the way they are voluntarily, and certainly aren't meaning to hurt us purposely. That's why we need to constantly remind ourselves to look at them as a whole person, and resentment or blame has no place there.

In supporting and advocating our loved one, it's vital for us to take time out for ourselves too. It can be exhausting and draining sometimes, and we need time away from the situation, so we continue feeling okay about the whole thing. We need to remember the importance of maintaining our own wellbeing, which we'll go further with in the next chapter.

CHAPTER 6

Putting it All Together–BPD the Holistic Way

You gain strength, courage, and confidence by every experience in which you really stop to look fear in the face. You must do the things which you think you cannot do.

–Eleanor Roosevelt

At this point, it should be clearer what BPD is, what it isn't, and what it's really like to care for a person with this condition. Although we've given many suggestions and tips that can be incorporated into a current treatment plan, there are some other valuable methods that can also be considered. The holistic approach to any form of health has many valuable options that our loved one may embrace and practice more freely than therapy practices recommended for them alone. The main reason for their draw to the holistic is that they are treated more as a whole person with different components that each need care, rather than simply a mentally ill person.

The initial step would be to work with our loved one on mindfulness. We've brought this up in earlier chapters, but we're going to go much deeper. For a person who spends much of their time in the past, and worrying endlessly about what will come, the best gift we as supporters can offer to our loved one is how to live in the present. That means grasping the concept of living today, being open-minded to the benefits of living a mindful life, and techniques and exercises the person can do on their own. It's essential for them to learn this mindset so they're finally able to let go of what is holding them back, being strong enough to let go of the negatives, and to put effective tools into play whenever they feel overwhelmed or drawn to old ways of coping.

Next is incorporating mental toughness with mindfulness. The two go hand-in-hand because one is living life for today, while the other are the things we put into practice to get past all of life's unpredictable, sometimes difficult, bumps. This is another important lesson for our loved ones because being mentally tough doesn't mean we forget about our past and the damage it's caused. It means that we acknowledge that it happened, and will find a way to make us better. As is the same with living with BPD, it's a part of who we are and with what's to come.

The important part of the holistic approach is solidifying the connection among the body, mind, and spirit. When one of these areas is out of sync, it tends to knock the entire system out of effective production. For those living with serious mental health issues, understanding this connection, and ways to strengthen it, will change how they see everything. It could make the difference between throwing the towel in, and persevering until everything seems brighter.

We'll end the chapter with final suggestions on how to inspire our loved one to carry on living their lives in the most productive way in spite of their BPD diagnosis. That is true powerfulness.

Being Mindful, Staying Mentally Tough, and Living Holistically

Mindfulness, for those who may not be familiar with it, is focusing our attention on the present moment, and the willingness to accept it without judgment. It's come to be seen as a key element in reducing stress and experiencing true happiness. From the viewpoint of a person supporting a loved one with BPD, this is exactly what most of us hope they achieve. But, like with any sort of life change, it takes a lot of constant and consistent work. It can prove to be invaluable if our loved one fully embraces this mindset. And once they do, being more mentally tough and holistically in sync will fall into place naturally.

The benefits of living mindfully are numerous that can bring calmness to many physical and psychological symptoms, as well as increase health, attitude, and benefits. It works by embracing a sense of acceptance about all experiences—good and bad—rather than to avoid dealing with them. The three most beneficial areas include improving:

- **well-being.** When we're mindful, we become more fully engaged in activities and it helps us deal with adverse events, situations, or people. We are also less likely to become obsessed with what might happen or what has happened, which helps us to do things that truly matter to us and where we want to be. This increases self-esteem and confidence, and develops deeper connections with others.

- **physical health.** Mindfulness has many health benefits including dealing with stress better, lowering heart disease, lowering blood pressure, eases chronic pain, improves sleep patterns, and helps to improve the gastrointestinal system. Basically, the idea of lowering stress, worry, and concern about things beyond our control helps to alleviate the negative physical symptoms stemming from stress.

- **mental health.** Many psychotherapists have incorporated mindful meditation practices into their therapy plans as a positive coping tool for depression, substance abuse, eating disorders, anxiety disorders, and OCD. These are all conditions that tend to veer off the present path, and learning mindful practices can help switch our focus.

There are various ways of practicing mindfulness, and it's important to find a routine that works best. For a person living with BPD, this could be somewhat of a challenge as their needs and focuses seem to change often. Whatever technique, or combination of different ones, is chosen, the end goal should be achieving a state of alertness, focused relaxation, and acceptance of what's happening in the now. In that way, the person will be able to refocus on the present moment, no matter what other distractions are around them at the same time.

All mindful practices are some form of meditation, when we sit silently, focusing on natural breathing or on a 'mantra'. The idea is to allow thoughts to come and leave freely with no judgment or concern. There are specific areas to drift focus to as the loved one relaxes into their practice. The main ones include:

- **body sensations.** Some examples might be itching, tingling, shivers, or similar input. The idea is to allow them to come in, acknowledge them and how they affect the body, then let them pass. It's powerful to achieve because as we supporters know, it can be a tiny body sensation that doesn't feel right that can throw the BPD person into a whirlwind of negative reactions.

- **sensory input.** It isn't possible to tune out all sensory input because our world is filled with it. Remind the person to make mental note of all things that tap into our senses, name them as they're experienced, then release them.

- **emotions.** Our loved one with BPD is bombarded with emotions they often don't know how to process. In their meditative state, they should allow emotions and emotional responses to enter their space, name them as they come to the surface, then breathe through them as they let the emotions pass.

- **cravings or urges.** There are so many examples

in this area but for the sake of working with a person with BPD, the focus should be on cravings, behavior, and addictions. If any of these present themselves, guide the loved one to let them in so they can pay close attention to the way those things make their body feel. Once there, work them through it by wishing it away by replacing it with healthier thoughts, then help them let it go.

All of these sound easier to instruct, than to put into play but they can be done with the right aspiration and strength. They'll need help learning the basics in order to carry through on their own, and the main part is building a strong base of the ability to concentrate. Mindful meditation grows from this base of concentration skills and the practice of acceptance. Here are ways to guide them toward concentration and acceptance practices:

- **Go with it.** Once concentration is developed, the loved one will be able to connect effectively with their inner thoughts, sensations, and emotions without judging them as 'good' or 'bad.' This is an amazing realization to get to because the person would experience more sincere, happy moments that will overshadow the bad.

- **Focus.** Making themselves aware of the sensory input around them will help guide them to enjoy the moment as it is in a particular moment. It means those moments won't be tarnished with the 'then' or the 'what-ifs,' and they'll be able to distinguish between feelings of well-being and those that trigger anguish.

- **Perseverance.** Initially, our loved one may struggle with sitting still, taking in all sensations around them, and how their body responds to those things. If they stay with it, though, their perimeter of tolerance will expand a little bit each time. And if for any reason they miss or feel they aren't able to do a session, they should be encouraged to go back to it when they feel more receptive.

- **Ability to redirect with empathy.** After a while, our loved one will be able to sense when their mind is wandering off or shutting down, and they'll have the inner energy to guide them back to the moment.

Mindfulness meditation should be practiced at least 20 minutes at first, working the way up to 45 minutes. The goal is to work toward doing a session at a comfortable time six days a week. This is something that will need to be worked into since most people with BPD aren't able to focus on one thing, sit still for too long, or enjoy any of the bodily sensations. All we can do is encourage and guide them, or even do it right by their side, initially.

Becoming, and Staying, Mentally Tough

As we've learned, physical and mental health isn't innate. We have to work at it in order to develop it most effectively. Here are a few effective ways to guide our loved one to become mentally tough:

- **Practicing present-thinking.** We discussed this in the last section, but in terms of being mentally tough, the focus in this mindset is not shying away from difficult times or challenges, but to embrace them and all we're supposed to gain from them presently.

- **Our mind needs daily exercise, too.** Muscles need to strengthen and grow in order to be able to handle the next challenge. The same holds true for the mind. The strength of the mind is built through the small wins throughout the day, and to be confident with our choices. Our loved one will find it empowering to do tasks that stretch our mental capacity.

- **Embrace challenges.** The entire idea behind challenging themselves is to empower our BPD loved one with not just setting goals that are simple to reach. The idea is to challenge themselves with goals that they *might* achieve, but require the greatest effort. This grows from believing in ourselves and our abilities, which strengthens as each goal is met.

- **React positively.** This is a major component of mental toughness, and a trait that those with BPD need to learn. It can be humbling and difficult to realize that we may not have control over what happens around us sometimes, but we do have control over our responses. Our loved ones are slowly learning that they can't control others, and they'll be accomplishing amazing things once they're in tune with their reactions.

- **We are stronger than fear.** Our loved ones may not completely believe this most days but when they're resilient enough to face their fear, it will dissipate and so will its effect on them.

- **Remove 'can't' from our vocabulary.** The idea of mental toughness is to remove negative words we tend to believe over the positive ones that get us further on our life's journey. Anything is possible with the right attitude.

- **Perseverance means empowerment.** The idea of perseverance is not allowing hurdles to stop us from getting to where we want to be. Our loved one drowns in negative words that keep them down. Facing, and conquering, fear or bad moments without throwing the gloves down is inspiring.

- **Seek answers.** To get a handle on the voices they hear, which control their responses most of the time, is the bravest way to respond to stressors better.

- **Gratefulness.** There will always be a person who can do what we're doing a little bit better than we're able to. That's okay, but it's a difficult thing to accept for those living with BPD. There's no room for jealousy or anger. Our loved one needs to learn that even though there are people who do what they're able to do, the fear and self-doubt try seeping in the cracks. If we're grateful for who we are and what we're good at, we'll be happy and grateful for others too.

- **Prepare for the bad times.** Life isn't an easy ride so there will always be adversity and tough times to face. But if our loved one learns to prepare for these times, and knows how they can respond to them, they'll have an easier time.

- **Giving ourselves credit.** When moments of self-doubt arise, the best way to combat them is to remind our loved one all they've accomplished. One tough time won't eliminate those successful times, and those are what our loved one needs to hold onto.

- **Practice every day.** Reaching and maintaining mental toughness is a continuous, day-to-day effort. It's not going to just happen, and it won't stick if we leave it on the sidelines. Being in tune with ourselves, our reactions, and our goals will keep mental toughness strong.

All effort put into being more mentally tough is rewarded in countless ways, so we should make sure we're tapping into it constantly.

A Holistic Approach to Mental Health

The holistic approach is caring for ourselves as a whole person, rather than a cluster of symptoms. The idea is that when we aren't feeling right, this is usually because somewhere within the mind, body, and spirit connection there's an unbalance that seeps into the other areas. In other words, we're out of balance.

When we see the self as a whole, and treat it accordingly, we'll guide ourselves back into a balanced state and we'll feel better. This is particularly important for our loved ones with BPD who are vulnerable to not only falling out of sync, but in feeding off the negatives they feel rather than turning to their more positive coping methods. These are a few tips we can work with our loved one to achieve inner balance:

- **Value ourselves.** Remind them to turn off the tapes playing self-criticizing words, and focus more on kindness and respect for themself. Guide them to practicing their hobbies, making time for their favorite projects, and help them broaden their horizons through new experiences.

- **Value our body.** This point has been touched on earlier but doing all that's possible to maintain physical health as when it's ignored, it impacts mental health too. This includes eating healthy meals, drinking water, avoiding smoking/vaping, getting the body moving, and making sure they get enough rest.

- **Surround ourselves with good people.** It's important to have strong family and close friend connections. Knowing we're surrounded by those who accept us just the way we are, no matter what happens, makes us stronger in every way. Think of how important we are to our loved one. Don't we make them stronger to stay on track?

- **Give back.** Those with BPD are highly empathetic, and tend to gravitate to those who need a bit of extra help. Volunteering time serves a double purpose in that it gives them a way to meet new people (something they often avoid), and it just feels good.

- **Deal with stress effectively.** We've discussed this in great detail, but it's a strong element in the holistic approach. Stress is a part of life whether we like it or not. But if we guide our loved one to the best ways to cope with it, it won't be allowed to grow to the point of no return. With all the tactics we've touched on, there's one that's really effective: laughter. When we laugh we release 'feel good' hormones, we release built up stress, and it's fun. It's also contagious, in a good way.

- **Quiet the mind.** This is one of the toughest things for someone with BPD to do, but we've learned several ways to help them do this. Remind them to practice deep breathing, meditation, writing in a journal, or other ways they find will calm the mind. They need to drain their brain of excess noise.

- **Setting doable goals.** Goals need to be reachable, and have meaning to overall happiness. If goals are too easy, they may get bored and feel unchallenged. If they're too difficult, they'll be too frustrated to keep trying. Set goals that challenge, but keep them moving forward.

- **Insert little surprises in everyday routine.** Our loved ones need routine, but they can become mundane, boring, and uninspiring. Throwing a few tidbits of new help can breathe life into a routine and help to rejuvenate the person.

- **Say 'no' to drugs, alcohol, and other substances.** To put it simply, a person who already lives with a condition that wreaks havoc on their brain chemistry and their behavior, consuming substances that do the same thing but worse will only lead to disaster. If it's not prescribed by a healthcare provider, it shouldn't be put in their body.

- **Ask for help.** Whether it's reaching out to us, to a member of their mental health team, or another trusted person when they feel they're in the middle of a whirlwind, they should know when to ask for help. It's never a sign of weakness, but strength and courage.

Our loved ones are doing their very best to live in our world with skills we take for granted and they work so hard to practice. When they have the right tools, they are capable of doing everything they set their sights on, and to be an effective contributor to our community.

Chapter Summary

In our various discussions on BPD, the main goal was not just to elicit understanding about the condition itself, but more to embrace supporters trying to care for these individuals. Even the most serious and daunting ailments can be made easier to absorb when we understand them. Here's what was covered chapter-by-chapter.

Chapter One: If you're searching for help with how to support a person with BPD, you already have knowledge of the condition. This chapter goes into details about what it is, what it isn't, and how to see it even when the person tries their hardest to hide it. We go over the four different types of BPD, including the main signs of each and how they're similar and different.

Finally, we share how BPD feels from the perspective of those who live with it.

Chapter Two: This chapter goes into detail about the diagnostic process. Even though supporters share the same space as the sufferer, getting the right diagnosis can be a long, frustrating road. We talk about the different players on the mental health team, what they look for, and how they come to their diagnosis. There are often other comorbid conditions that make the whole process more difficult, and those are touched on too. We give supporters suggestions on things *not* to do with a loved one who has BPD, because we have to try not to feed into their manipulative nature. Finally, we compare and contrast the condition BPD is most often misdiagnosed as (and vice versa)—bipolar disorder.

Chapter Three: Once a diagnosis has been established, the next step is putting together the most effective treatment plan for the individual. There is no cure for BPD, but it *can* be treated effectively through a combination of medicinal and therapeutic methods. We go over the most common treatments. The chapter ends on a behavior called *splitting* that we supporters know is a sign that our loved one is moving into the beginning of an episode. Knowing what to watch for, what the person is really trying to say, and how to respond are so important in supporting, helping, and advocating for them.

Chapter Four: Now that we have a diagnosis and a solid treatment/therapy plan in place, now we can re-learn how to love the sufferer with and aside from their condition. After all, they're not BPD, they're a person learning to live with it. We'll give supporters strategies and suggestions to maintain our love and support through those stormy times. The supporters need support themselves, so we talk about some self-care for them. Finally, we may not realize it but there are actually positives about BPD, which remind us of the other parts of the individual that remain constant and good.

Chapter Five: When supporting a person with BPD, there's a lot of healing that will be in play. It's not just the person being treated for BPD that needs to heal, we as their allies and greatest supporters also need to heal. The entire support team needs to heal and let go of things as we move forward. Another area discussed is eliciting the importance of self-care in the sufferer, and giving them the tools they'll need to break the stigma many still have over those living with mental health issues. Through us, they'll learn how to advocate for themselves. Finally, we talk about strategies to put into play when the person resists or tries stopping treatment.

Chapter Six: The most important aspect of treatment/therapy for any condition is learning and maintaining the holistic approach. This involves the balance of the mind, body, and spirit connection, and seeing the person as a whole being made up of various elements. The focus in this chapter is offering suggestions with teaching the individual how to live life mindfully, embracing a mentally tough mindset, and maintain the whole self by living holistically.

CONCLUSION

Moving Forward Fearlessly

You are the one thing in this world, above all other things, that you must never give up on. When I was in middle school, I was struggling with severe anxiety and depression and the help and support I received from my family and a therapist saved my life. Asking for help is the first step. You are more precious to this world than you'll ever know.

–Lili Reinhart

The journey we've taken you on throughout our discussions may have been difficult. It's not to say that it wasn't familiar, because as the supporter of a person with BPD, we are all experts on our experience with this condition. We may not have the inside scoop, so to speak, that our loved one does but simply by being right by their side, we've seen how they suffer.

We've talked them down when that condition has taken them to a realm of distraught that consumes them. We take care of them when they're so far down, we're terrified to leave them alone. We've used our inner strength to breathe some purpose into their deflated self-worth, and offered our own life force to give them courage they don't have. We've taken the tools of self-harm away so they don't hurt themselves; we've chased them down the street when they can't take it anymore; we sleep on the floor by their bed or outside their door, so they won't escape our ever-watching eye; and we stay by their side when they try ending their pain. *That* is BPD. But it doesn't tell outsiders what it's really like, or how it really feels.

One of the most prominent reasons those with mental health conditions as serious as BPD don't seek the help they need is because of the stigma society still puts on mental illness. Sadly, it's what many people do when there is a lack of digestible information they can draw from to make a more educated perspective. And even when they're willing to take in that information, they still need to be open-minded enough to embrace and accept the person as *someone living with mental health struggles*. Just because an individual has a specific diagnosis, they should never be defined by it. Yet we still struggle with that line of thinking even in these modern times.

Through our discussions, suggestions, and tips presented in these chapters, we hope we've given supporters the voice they may not always have had to advocate for their loved one. Every effort we've made to keep our loved one facing forwards, whether they say they wanted us there or not, is rewarded hundreds of times when they pick themselves up and reach for our hand.

A person who has been supported, loved, and treated as a whole person will develop the courage to advocate for themselves. It *will* happen. Maybe not today, or even tomorrow, but it will.

Our Gratitude for Our Loved One's BPD Diagnosis

In Chapter Four, we touched on a few of the positive traits those with BPD have, and that we should celebrate in them. An amazing extension on this point is that these incredible people have a certain level of gratitude for their BPD diagnosis. That may sound somewhat contradictory after learning all the ins and outs of this condition. But when we get to the point where we can actually see the positives buried within the darkness of a very difficult mental health condition, it means the baton of power has changed. The person goes from "being controlled" by that invisible force to "being in control" of themselves, and that's powerful.

Gratitude is learned from coping with BPD, which may not always be practiced but it helps the person get through the tough days, appreciate tiny things in the good ones, and anything in between. Acknowledging even small things we have to be grateful for is a sign of hope that they need to hold on to. With hope, they can accomplish anything that falls in their path, then gratitude for getting through it as unscathed as possible.

That all being said, we'd like to leave off with a few specific points to remind our loved ones of what they should be proud of themselves for, ironically stemming directly from their BPD. Those are having gratitude for:

- **those they've met along their journey with BPD.** It's not just us who are by their sides whenever we're needed. They'll have an army of peers from their therapy sessions, the practitioners, the therapists, nurses, doctors, counselors, helpers on the therapy team, and the list goes on. They may have never met any of these people in any other avenue of life if they didn't share the core focus of BPD. This elite group of people truly understand what this condition is, and what it takes to survive the fights and the all-out battles. It's a gift to walk a line with other people who are doing the best they can, and making it work.

- **a sense of spirituality.** This is something learned during the holistic approach, and the alternative forms of treatment used. Spirituality doesn't necessarily mean religion. It's a connection with a force that is outside of ourselves, and bigger than we are. That connection brings us a sense of inner peace, balance, and connection to the world that we often feel disconnected from. BPD, then, can be seen as a source for this part of our whole self.

- **the other creative gifts that bring us completion and purpose.** Even if the individual has written, painted, played an instrument, sang, or whichever creative path they're on prior to their diagnosis, it intensifies. The person is taught to turn to and draw from these gifts to work through their difficult emotions, thoughts, and behavior and stop the immediate move from thought to response. For example, the person will become consumed with self-hate and not see the point in continuing life. Rather than taking permanent action, they open their journal and write through the thoughts and the feelings attached to them. Once the pen is laid down and the book closed, those thoughts may not be as prominent anymore. Creative gifts can literally save our loved one, and give them a sense of purpose and light.

There are so many examples of gratitude, which look different from each person living with BPD. What one person is grateful for isn't the same as for another. There may even be those who aren't at the point to see any gratitude or positivity in their condition. This could be something else to guide them to work on as it's a beautiful source of inspiration, empowerment, and strength to look back on.

Thank You

Before you leave, I'd just like to say, thank you so much for purchasing my book.

I spent many days and nights working on this book so I could finally put this in your hands.

So, before you leave, I'd like to ask you a small favor.

Would you please consider posting a review on the platform? Your reviews are one of the best ways to support indie authors like me, and every review counts.

Your feedback will allow me to continue writing books just like this one, so let me know if you enjoyed it and why. I read every review and I would love to hear from you. Simply visit the link below to leave a review.

References

Alexander, K. (2019, March 22). https://themighty.com/2019/03/facts-about-life-with-borderline-personalNot much covered was unfamiliar because there may have been more familiarityity-disorder-bpd/?utm_source=yahoo&utm_medium=referral&utm_ca mpaign=in-story-related-link

Churchill, A. (2021, November 5). *Nine Strategies for Supporting Someone with BPD* https://ca.ctrinstitute.com/blog/9-strategies-supporting-bpd/

Clearview Treatment Programs. (July 20, 2018). https://www.clearviewtreatment.com/resources/blog/bipo lar-bpd-difference/

Daskal, L. (2018, June 10). *How to Make Yourself Mentally Strong This Year* https://www.lollydaskal.com/leadership/how-to-make-yourself-mentally-strong-this-year/

Easton, W. (2018). *I Am Grateful for My Borderline Personality Disorder*
https://www.healthyplace.com/blogs/borderline/2018/12
/i-am-grateful-for-my-borderline-personality-disorder

Fink, J. (February 18, 2020). *How Doctors Diagnose Borderline Personality Disorder.* https://www.healthgrades.com/right-care/mental-health-and-behavior/how-doctors-diagnose-borderline-personality-disorder

Fletcher, J. (2022, February 24). *Borderline Personality Disorder.* https://www.healthline.com/health/borderline-personality-disorder#complications

Fruzzetti, A. E. (2017). *Why Borderline Personality Disorder is Misdiagnosed* https://www.nami.org/Blogs/NAMI-Blog/October-2017/Why-Borderline-Personality-Disorder-is-Misdiagnose

Garrett, S. (2018). *11 Things People With Borderline Personality Disorder Do That Mean "I'm Splitting."* https://www.yahoo.com/lifestyle/11-things-people-borderline-personality-213213479.html

Harvard Health–Help Guide (December 4, 2018). *Benefits of Mindfulness.* https://www.helpguide.org/harvard/benefits-of-mindfulness.htm

Mighty, T. (May 22, 2018). https://themighty.com/2018/05/borderline-personality-disorder-bpd-i-need-help/

Greenstein, L. (June 23, 2017). *Supporting Someone with Borderline Personality Disorder* https://www.nami.org/Blogs/NAMI-Blog/June-2017/Supporting-Someone-with-Borderline-Personality-Dis

Michigan University Health Centre (2022). *Ten Things You Can Do for Your Mental Health* https://uhs.umich.edu/tenthings

NEA.BPD. (2014, February). *National Education Alliance for Borderline Personality Disorder.* https://www.borderlinepersonalitydisorder.org/what-is-bpd/bpd-overview/

Pugle, M. (2012). *What Are the Types of Borderline Personality Disorder?* https://www.verywellhealth.com/types-of-bpd-5193843

Salters-Pedneault, K. (2020). *Why Many People With Borderline Personality Disorder* Refuse Treatment. https://www.verywellmind.com/when-your-loved-one-is-refusing-treatment-425198#:~:text=If%20you%20or%20a%20loved,see%20our%20National%20Helpline%20Database.

Self-care for BPD. (2018). https://www.mind.org.uk/information-support/types-of-mental-health-problems/borderline-personality-disorder-bpd/self-care-for-bpd/

Smith, M. (2018, November 3). Helping Someone with Borderline Personality Disorder.

https://www.helpguide.org/articles/mental-disorders/helping-someone-with-borderline-personality-disorder.htm

Made in the USA
Las Vegas, NV
18 January 2024

84575797R00090